POEMS FOR CHI.

BY

CELIA THAXTER

WITH ILLUSTRATIONS BY MISS A. G. PLYMPTON

BOSTON
HOUGHTON, MIFFLIN AND COMPANY
New York : 11 East Seventeenth Street
The Riverside Press, Cambridge
1884

The Riverside Press, Cambridge:
Electrotyped and Printed by H. O. Houghton & Co.

THE SANDPIPER.

CONTENTS.

CONTENTS.

LIST OF FULL-PAGE ILLUSTRATIONS.

THE SANDPIPER.

IT was such a pretty nest, and in such a pretty place, I must tell you about it.

One lovely afternoon in May I had been wandering up and down, through rocky gorges, by little swampy bits of ground, and on the tops of windy headlands, looking for flowers, and had found many : large blue violets, the like of which you never saw ; white violets, too, creamy and fragrant ; gentle little houstonias ; gay and dancing erythroniums ; and wind flowers delicately tinted, blue, straw-color, pink, and purple. I never found such in the mainland valleys. The salt air of the sea deepens the colors of all flowers. I stopped by a swamp which the recent rains had filled and turned into a little lake. Light green iris-leaves cut the water like sharp and slender swords, and, in the low sunshine that streamed across, threw long shadows over the shining surface. Some blackbirds were calling sweetly in a clump of bushes, and song-sparrows sung as if they had but one hour in which to crowd the whole rapture of the spring. As I pressed through the budding bayberry bushes to reach some milk-white sprays of shad-

1

bush which grew by the water side, I startled three cur-
lews. They flew away, trailing their long legs, and
whistling fine and clear. I stood still to watch them
out of sight. How full the air was of pleasant sounds!
The very waves made a glad noise about the rocks, and
the whole sea seemed to roar afar off, as if half asleep
and murmuring in a kind of gentle dream. The flock
of sheep was scattered here and there, all washed as
white as snow by the plenteous rains, and nibbling the
new grass eagerly ; and from near and far came the
tender and plaintive cries of the young lambs.

Going on again, I came to the edge of a little beach,
and presently I was startled by a sound of such terror
and distress that it went to my heart at once. In a
moment a poor little sandpiper emerged from the
bushes, dragging itself along in such a way that, had
you seen it, you would have concluded that every bone
in its body had been broken. Such a dilapidated bird !
Its wings drooped, and its legs hung as if almost lifeless. It uttered continually a shrill cry of pain, and
kept just out of the reach of my hand, fluttering hither
and thither as if sore wounded and weary. At first I
was amazed, and cried out, "Why, friend and gossip!
what *is* the matter ?" and then stood watching it in
mute dismay. Suddenly it flashed across me that this
was only my sandpiper's way of concealing from me a
nest ; and I remembered reading about this little trick
of hers in a book of Natural History. The object was
to make me follow her by pretending she could not fly,

and so lead me away from her treasure. So I stood perfectly still, lest I should tread on the precious habitation, and quietly observed my deceitful little friend. Her apparently desperate and hopeless condition grew so comical when I reflected that it was only affectation, that I could not help laughing loud and long. "Dear gossip," I called to her, "pray don't give yourself so much unnecessary trouble ! You might know I would n't hurt you or your nest for the world, you most absurd of birds ! " As if she understood me, and as if she could not brook being ridiculed, up she rose at once, strong and graceful, and flew off with a full, round, clear note, delicious to hear.

Then I cautiously looked for the nest, and found it quite close to my feet, near the stem of a stunted bayberry-bush. Mrs. Sandpiper had only drawn together a few bayberry-leaves, brown and glossy, a little pale green lichen, and a twig or two, and that was a pretty enough house for her. Four eggs, about as large as robins', were within, all laid evenly with the small ends together, as is the tidy fashion of the Sandpiper family. No wonder I did not see them ; for they were pale green like the lichen, with brown spots the color of the leaves and twigs, and they seemed a part of the ground, with its confusion of soft neutral tints. I could n't admire them enough, but, to relieve my little friend's anxiety, I came very soon away ; and as I came, I marveled much that so very small a head should contain such an amount of cunning.

THE SANDPIPER.

Across the narrow beach we flit,
   One little sandpiper and I ;
And fast I gather, bit by bit,
   The scattered driftwood bleached and dry.
The wild waves reach their hands for it,
   The wild wind raves, the tide runs high,
As up and down the beach we flit, —
   One little sandpiper and I.

Above our heads the sullen clouds
   Scud black and swift across the sky ;
Like silent ghosts in misty shrouds
   Stand out the white light-houses high.
Almost as far as eye can reach
   I see the close-reefed vessels fly,
As fast we flit along the beach, —
   One little sandpiper and I.

I watch him as he skims along
   Uttering his sweet and mournful cry ;
He starts not at my fitful song,
   Or flash of fluttering drapery.

He has no thought of any wrong;
  He scans me with a fearless eye.
Stanch friends are we, well tried and strong,
  The little sandpiper and I.

Comrade, where wilt thou be to-night
  When the loosed storm breaks furiously?
My driftwood fire will burn so bright!
  To what warm shelter canst thou fly?
I do not fear for thee, though wroth
  The tempest rushes through the sky:
For are we not God's children both,
  Thou, little sandpiper, and I?

SPRING.

THE alder by the river
  Shakes out her powdery curls;
The willow buds in silver
  For little boys and girls.

The little birds fly over,
  And O, how sweet they sing!
To tell the happy children
  That once again 't is spring.

The gay green grass comes creeping
  So soft beneath their feet;
The frogs begin to ripple
  A music clear and sweet.

And buttercups are coming,
  And scarlet columbine,
And in the sunny meadows
  The dandelions shine.

And just as many daisies
  As their soft hands can hold
The little ones may gather,
  All fair in white and gold.

Here blows the warm red
   clover,
There peeps the violet
   blue ;
O happy little children !
God made them all for
   you.

THE BURGOMASTER GULL.

THE old-wives sit on the heaving brine,
   White-breasted in the sun,
Preening and smoothing their feathers fine,
   And scolding, every one.

The snowy kittiwakes overhead,
   With beautiful beaks of gold,
And wings of delicate gray outspread,
   Float, listening while they scold.

And a foolish guillemot, swimming by,
   Though heavy and clumsy and dull,
Joins in with a will when he hears their cry
   'Gainst the Burgomaster Gull.

For every sea-bird, far and near,
   With an atom of brains in its skull,
Knows plenty of reasons for hate and fear
   Of the Burgomaster Gull.

The black ducks gather, with plumes so rich,
   And the coots in twinkling lines ;
And the swift and slender water-witch,
   Whose neck like silver shines ;

Big eider-ducks, with their caps pale green
  And their salmon-colored vests ;
And gay mergansers sailing between,
  With their long and glittering crests.

But the loon aloof on the outer edge
  Of the noisy meeting keeps,
And laughs to watch them behind the ledge
  Where the lazy breaker sweeps.

They scream and wheel, and dive and fret,
  And flutter in the foam ;
And fish and mussels blue they get
  To feed their young at home :

Till hurrying in, the little auk
  Brings tidings that benumbs,
And stops at once their clamorous talk, —
  " The Burgomaster comes !"

And up he sails, a splendid sight !
  With " wings like banners " wide,
And eager eyes both big and bright,
  That peer on every side.

A lovely kittiwake flying past
  With a slippery pollock fine, —
Quoth the Burgomaster, " Not so fast,
  My beauty ! This is mine !"

His strong wing strikes with a dizzying shock;
    Poor kittiwake, shrieking, flees;
His booty he takes to the nearest rock,
    To eat it at his ease.

The scared birds scatter to left and right,
    But the bold buccaneer, in his glee,
Cares little enough for their woe and their fright, —
    "'T will be *your* turn next!" cries he.

He sees not, hidden behind the rock,
    In the sea-weed, a small boat's hull,
Nor dreams he the gunners have spared the flock
    For the Burgomaster Gull.

So proudly his dusky wings are spread,
    And he launches out on the breeze, —
When lo! what thunder of wrath and dread!
    What deadly pangs are these!

The red blood drips and the feathers fly,
    Down drop the pinions wide;
The robber-chief, with a bitter cry,
    Falls headlong in the tide!

They bear him off with laugh and shout;
    The wary birds return, —
From the clove-brown feathers that float about
    The glorious news they learn.

Then such a tumult fills the place
　As never was sung or said ;
And all cry, wild with joy, " The base,
　Bad Burgomaster 's dead ! "

And the old-wives sit with their caps so white,
　And their pretty beaks so red,
And swing on the billows, and scream with delight,
　For the Burgomaster 's dead !

LITTLE GUSTAVA.

Little Gustava sits in the sun,
Safe in the porch, and the little drops run
From the icicles under the eaves so fast,
For the bright spring sun shines warm at last,
　　And glad is little Gustava.

She wears a quaint little scarlet cap,
And a little green bowl she holds in her lap,
Filled with bread and milk to the brim,
And a wreath of marigolds round the rim :
　　" Ha, ha ! " laughs little Gustava.

Up comes her little gray, coaxing cat,
With her little pink nose, and she mews, " What's
　　that ? "

Gustava feeds her, — she begs for more ;
And a little brown hen walks in at the door :
    " Good-day ! " cries little Gustava.

She scatters crumbs for the little brown hen.
There comes a rush and a flutter, and then
Down fly her little white doves so sweet,
With their snowy wings and their crimson feet:
    "Welcome!" cries little Gustava.

So dainty and eager they pick up the crumbs,
But who is this through the door-way comes?
Little Scotch terrier, little dog Rags,
Looks in her face, and his funny tail wags:
    "Ha, ha!" laughs little Gustava.

"You want some breakfast, too?" and down
She sets her bowl on the brick floor brown;
And little dog Rags drinks up her milk,
While she strokes his shaggy locks, like silk:
    "Dear Rags!" says little Gustava.

Waiting without stood sparrow and crow,
Cooling their feet in the melting snow:
"Won't you come in, good folk?" she cried.
But they were too bashful, and stayed outside,
    Though "Pray come in!" cried Gustava.

So the last she threw them, and knelt on the mat
With doves and biddy and dog and cat.
And her mother came to the open house-door:
"Dear little daughter, I bring you some more,
    My merry little Gustava!"

Kitty and terrier, biddy and doves,
All things harmless Gustava loves.
The shy, kind creatures 't is joy to feed,
And oh, her breakfast is sweet indeed
    To happy little Gustava!

CHANTICLEER.

I WAKE! I feel the day is near;
  I hear the red cock crowing!
He cries "'T is dawn!" How sweet and clear
His cheerful call comes to my ear,
  While light is slowly growing.

The white snow gathers, flake on flake;
  I hear the red cock crowing!
Is anybody else awake
To see the winter morning break,
  While thick and fast 't is snowing?

I think the world is all asleep;
  I hear the red cock crowing!
Out of the frosty pane I peep;
The drifts are piled so wide and deep,
  And wild the wind is blowing!

Nothing I see has shape or form;
  I hear the red cock crowing!

But that dear voice comes through the storm
To greet me in my nest so warm,
  As if the sky were glowing!

A happy little child, I lie
  And hear the red cock crowing.
The day is dark. I wonder why
His voice rings out so brave and high,
  With gladness overflowing.

THE WATER-BLOOM.

A CHILD looked up in the summer sky
Where a soft, bright shower had just passed by;
Eastward the dusk rain-curtain hung,
And swiftly across it the rainbow sprung.

" Papa! papa! what is it?" she cried,
As she gazed with her blue eyes opened wide
At the wonderful arch that bridged the heaven,
Vividly glowing with colors seven.

"Why, that is the rainbow, darling child."
And the father down on his baby smiled.
"What makes it, papa?" "The sun, my dear,
That shines on the water-drops so clear."

Here was a beautiful mystery !
No more questions to ask had she,
But she thought the garden's loveliest flowers
Had floated upward and caught in the showers —

Rose, violet, orange marigold —
In a ribbon of light on the clouds unrolled !
Red of poppy, and green leaves too,
Sunflower yellow, and larkspur blue.

A great, wide, wondrous, splendid wreath
It seemed to the little girl beneath ;
How did it grow so fast up there,
And suddenly blossom, high in the air ?

She could not take her eyes from the sight :
" Oh, look !" she cried in her deep delight,
As she watched the glory spanning the gloom,
" Oh, look at the beautiful water-bloom !"

CROCUS.

Oh the dear, delightful sound
Of the drops that to the ground
From the eaves rejoicing run
In the February sun!
Drip, drip, drip, they slide and slip
From the icicles' bright tip,
Till they melt the sullen snow
On the garden bed below.
"Bless me! what is all this drumming?"
Cries the crocus, "I am coming!
Pray don't knock so long and loud,
For I'm neither cross nor proud.
But a little sleepy still,
With the winter's lingering chill.
Never mind! 'T is time to wake,
Through the dream at last to break!"
'T is as quickly done as said,
Up she thrusts her golden head,
Looks about with radiant eyes
In a kind of shy surprise,
Tries to say in accents surly,
"Well! you called me very early!"
But she lights with such a smile
All the darksome place the while,

2

Every heart begins to stir
Joyfully at sight of her;
Every creature grows more gay
Looking in her face to-day.
She is greeted, "Welcome, dear!
Fresh smile of the hopeful year!
First bright print of Spring's light feet,
Golden crocus, welcome, sweet!"
And she whispers, looking up
From her richly glowing cup,
At the sunny eaves so high
Overhead against the sky,
"Now I've come, O sparkling drops,
All your clattering, pattering stops.
And I'm very glad I came,
And you're not the least to blame
That you hammered at the snow
Till you wakened me below
With your one incessant tune.
I'm not here a bit too soon!"

THE CONSTANT DOVE.

THE white dove sat on the sunny eaves,
And " What will you do when the north wind
    grieves ? "
She said to the busy nuthatch small,
Tapping above in the gable tall.

He probed each crack with his slender beak,
And much too busy he was to speak.
Spiders, that thought themselves safe and sound,
And moths and flies and cocoons he found.

Oh ! but the white dove she was fair,
Bright she shone in the autumn air,
Turning her head from the left to the right;
Only to watch her was such delight !

" Coo !" she murmured, " poor little thing,
What will you do when the frosts shall sting ?
Spiders and flies will be hidden or dead,
Snow underneath and snow overhead."

Nuthatch paused in his busy care:
" And what will *you* do, O white dove fair ? "

" Oh, kind hands feed me with crumbs and grain,
And I wait with patience for spring again."

He laughed so loud that his laugh I heard.
" How can you be such a stupid bird!
What are your wings for, tell me, pray,
But to bear you from tempests and cold away?

" Merrily off to the South I fly,
In search of the summer, presently,
And warmth and beauty I'll find anew.
Why don't you follow the summer, too?"

But she cooed content on the sunny eaves,
And looked askance at the reddening leaves;
And grateful I whispered: " O white dove true,
I'll feed you and love you the winter through."

THE WANING MOON.

THE moon is tired and old ;
In the morning darkness cold
She drifts up the paling sky,
With cheek flushed wearily.

A little longer, and lo!
She is lost in the sun's bright glow;
A thin shell, pearly and pale,
'Mid soft white clouds that sail.

Art faint and sad, dear moon?
Gladness shall find thee soon!
Sorry art thou to wane?
Thou shalt be young again!

And beautiful as before
Thou shalt live in the sky once more ;
From the baby crescent small
Thou shalt grow to the golden ball:

And again will the children shout,
"Oh look at the moon, look out!"
For thou shalt be great and bright
As when God first made night.

THE BIRDS' ORCHESTRA.

BOBOLINK shall play the violin,
 Great applause to win;
Lonely, sweet, and sad, the meadow lark
 Plays the oboe.   Hark!
That inspired bugle with a soul —
 'T is the oriole;
Yellow-bird the clarionet shall play,
 Blithe, and clear, and gay.
Purple finch what instrument will suit?
 He can play the flute.
Fire-winged blackbirds sound the merry fife,
 Soldiers without strife;
And the robins wind the mellow horn
 Loudly eve and morn.
Who shall clash the cymbals?   Jay and crow;
 That is all they know.
Hylas twang their harps so weird and high,
 Such a tuneful cry!
And to roll the deep, melodious drum,
 Lo! the bull-frogs come!
Then the splendid chorus, who shall sing
 Of so fine a thing?

Who the names of the performers call
    Truly, one and all ?
Blue-bird, bunting, cat-bird, chickadee
    (Phœbe-bird is he),
Swallow, creeper, cross-bill, cuckoo, dove,
    Wee wren that I love;
Brisk fly-catcher, finches — what a crowd !
    King-bird whistling loud ;
Sweet rose-breasted grossbeak, vireo, thrush —
    Hear these two, and hush ;
Scarlet tanager, song-sparrow small
    (Dearer he than all;
At the first sound of his friendly voice
    Saddest hearts rejoice),
Redpoll, nuthatch, thrasher, plover gray —
    Curlew did I say ?
What a jangling all the grakles make !
    Is it some mistake ?
Anvil chorus yellow-hammers strike,
    And the wicked shrike
Harshly creaks like some half-open door ;
    He can do no more.

NIKOLINA.

OH TELL me, little children, have you seen her —
The tiny maid from Norway, Nikolina?
Oh, her eyes are blue as corn flowers 'mid the corn,
And her cheeks are rosy red as skies of morn!

Oh buy the baby's blossoms if you meet her,
And stay with gentle words and looks to greet her;
She'll gaze at you and smile and clasp your hand,
But no word of your speech can understand.

Nikolina! Swift she turns if any call her,
As she stands among the poppies hardly taller,
Breaking off their flaming scarlet cups for you,
With spikes of slender larkspur, brightly blue.

In her little garden many a flower is growing —
Red, gold, and purple in the soft wind blowing;
But the child that stands amid the blossoms gay
Is sweeter, quainter, brighter even than they.

Oh tell me, little children, have you seen her —
This baby girl from Norway, Nikolina?
Slowly she's learning English words, to try
And thank you if her flowers you come to buy.

NIKOLINA.

MILKING

LITTLE dun cow to the apple-tree tied,
  Chewing the cud of reflection,
I that am milking you, sit by your side,
  Lost in a sad retrospection.

Far o'er the field the tall daisies blush warm,
  For rosy the sunset is dying;
Across the still valley, o'er meadow and farm,
  The flush of its beauty is lying.

White foams the milk in the pail at my feet,
  Clearly the robins are calling;
Soft blows the evening wind after the heat,
  Cool the long shadows are falling.

Little dun cow, 't is so tranquil and sweet!
  Are you light-hearted, I wonder?
What do *you* think about, — something to eat?
  On clover and grass do you ponder?

I am remembering days that are dead,
  And a brown little maid in the gloaming,
Milking her cow, with the west burning red
  Over waves that about her were foaming.

Up from the sad east the deep shadows gloomed
    Out of the distance and found her ;
Lightly she sang while the solemn sea boomed
    Like a great organ around her.

Under the light-house no sweet-brier grew,
    Dry was the grass, and no daisies
Waved in the wind, and the flowers were few
    That lifted their delicate faces.

But oh, she was happy, and careless, and blest,
    Full of the song-sparrow's spirit ;
Grateful for life, for the least and the best
    Of the blessings that mortals inherit.

Fairer than gardens of Paradise seemed
    The desolate spaces of water ;
Nature was hers, — clouds that frowned — stars
        that gleamed, —
    What beautiful lessons they taught her !

Would I could find you again, little maid,
    Striving with utmost endeavor, —
Could find in my breast that light heart, unafraid,
    That has vanished for ever and ever !

YELLOW-BIRD.

YELLOW-BIRD, where did you learn that song,
  Perched on the trellis where grape-vines clamber,
In and out fluttering, all day long,
  With your golden breast bedropped with amber?

Where do you hide such a store of delight,
  O delicate creature, tiny and slender,
Like a mellow morning sunbeam bright
  And overflowing with music tender!

You never learned it at all, the song
  . Springs from your heart in rich completeness,
Beautiful, blissful, clear and strong,
  Steeped in the summer's ripest sweetness.

To think we are neighbors of yours! How fine!
  Oh what a pleasure to watch you together,
Bringing your fern-down and floss to re-line
  The nest worn thin by the winter weather!

Send up your full notes like worshipful prayers;
  Yellow-bird, sing while the summer's before you;
Little you dream that, in spite of their cares,
  Here's a whole family, proud to adore you!

A TRIUMPH.

LITTLE ROGER up the long slope rushing
    Through the rustling corn,
Showers of dew-drops from the broad leaves
      brushing
    In the early morn,

At his sturdy little shoulder bearing,
    For a banner gay,
Stem of fir with one long shaving flaring
    In the wind away!

Up he goes, the summer sunrise flushing
    O'er him in his race,
Sweeter dawn of rosy childhood blushing
    On his radiant face;

If he can but set his standard glorious
    On the hill-top low,
Ere the sun climbs the clear sky victorious,
    All the world aglow!

So he presses on with childish ardor,
    Almost at the top!
Hasten, Roger! Does the way grow harder?
    Wherefore do you stop?

From below the corn-stalks tall and slender
    Comes a plaintive cry;
Turns he for an instant from the splendor
    Of the crimson sky,

Wavers, then goes flying toward the hollow,
    Calling loud and clear,
"Coming, Jenny! Oh, why did you follow?
    Don't you cry, my dear!"

Small Janet sits weeping 'mid the daisies;
    "Little sister sweet,
Must you follow Roger?" Then he raises
    Baby on her feet.

Guides her tiny steps with kindness tender,
    Cheerfully and gay,
All his courage and his strength would lend her
    Up the uneven way,

Till they front the blazing east together;
    But the sun has rolled
Up the sky in the still summer weather,
    Flooding them with gold.

All forgotten is the boy's ambition,
    Low the standard lies,
Still they stand, and gaze — a sweeter vision
    Ne'er met mortal eyes.

That was splendid, Roger, that was glorious,
    Thus to help the weak;
Better than to plant your flag victorious
    On earth's highest peak!

SLUMBER SONG.

Thou little child, with tender, clinging arms,
    Drop thy sweet head, my darling, down and rest
Upon my shoulder, rest with all thy charms;
    Be soothed and comforted, be loved and blessed.

Against thy silken, honey-colored hair
    I lean a loving cheek, a mute caress;
Close, close I gather thee and kiss thy fair
    White eyelids, sleep so softly doth oppress.

Dear little face, that lies in calm content
    Within the gracious hollow that God made
In every human shoulder, where He meant
    Some tired head for comfort should be laid!

Most like a heavy-folded rose thou art,
    In summer air reposing, warm and still.
Dream thy sweet dreams upon my quiet heart;
    I watch thy slumber; naught shall do thee ill.

A TRIUMPH.

WARNING.

TAKE heed, O youth, both brave and bright,
Battles there are for you to fight !
Stand up erect and face them all,
Nor turning flee, nor wavering fall.
Of all the world's bewildering gifts,
Take only what the soul uplifts.
Keep firm your hand upon the helm
Lest bitter tempests overwhelm ;
And watch lest evil mists should mar
The glory of your morning star,
And robe the glory of the day
You have not reached, in sullen gray.
Choose then, O youth, both bright and brave !
Wilt be a monarch or a slave ?
Ah, scorn to take one step below
The paths where truth and honor go !
On manhood's threshold stand, a king,
Demanding all that life can bring
Of lofty thought, of purpose high,
Of beauty and nobility.
Once master of yourself, no fate
Can make your rich world desolate,
And all men shall look up to see
The glory of your victory.

THE BUTCHER-BIRD.

I 'LL tell you a story, children,
  The saddest you ever heard,
About Rupert, the pet canary,
  And a terrible butcher-bird.

There was such a blinding snow-storm
  One could not see at all,
And all day long the children
  Had watched the white flakes fall;

And when the eldest brothers
  Had kissed mamma good-night,
And up the stairs together
  Had gone with their bedroom light,

Of a sudden their two fresh voices
  Rang out in a quick surprise,
"Mamma! papa! come quickly
  And catch him before he flies!"

On a picture-frame perched lightly,
  With his head beneath his wing,
They had found a gray bird sitting;
  That was a curious thing!

Down stairs to the cosy parlor
   They brought him, glad to find
For the storm-tossed wanderer shelter;
   Not knowing his cruel mind!

And full of joy were the children
   To think he was safe and warm,
And had chosen their house for safety
   To hide from the raging storm!

" He shall stay with the pretty Rupert,
   And live among mother's flowers,
And he 'll sing with our robin and sparrow ; "
   And they talked about it for hours.

Alas, in the early morning
   There rose a wail and a cry,
And a fluttering wild in the cages,
   And Rupert's voice rang high.

We rushed to the rescue swiftly ;
   Too late! On the shining cage,
The home of the happy Rupert,
   All rough with fury and rage,

Stood the handsome, horrible stranger,
   With black and flashing eye,
And torn almost to pieces
   Did poor dead Rupert lie!

Oh, sad was all the household,
  And we mourned for Rupert long.
The fierce wild shrike was prisoned
  In a cage both dark and strong;

And would you like, O children,
  His final fate to know?
To Agassiz's Museum
  That pirate bird did go!

FERN-SEED.

SHE filled her shoes with fern-seed
  This foolish little Nell,
And in the summer sunshine
  Went dancing down the dell.
For whoso treads on fern-seed, —
  So fairy stories tell, —
Becomes invisible at once,
  So potent is its spell.
A frog mused by the brook-side :
  " Can you see me ? " she cried ;
He leaped across the water,
  A flying leap and wide.
" Oh that 's because I asked him !
  I must not speak," she thought,
And skipping o'er the meadow
  The shady wood she sought.
The squirrel chattered on the bough,
  Nor noticed her at all,
The birds sang high, the birds sang low,
  With many a cry and call.
The rabbit nibbled in the grass,
  The snake basked in the sun,
The butterflies, like floating flowers,
  Wavered and gleamed and shone.

The spider in his hammock swung,
 The gay grasshoppers danced ;
And now and then a cricket sung
 And shining beetles glanced.
'T was all because the pretty child
 So softly, softly trod, —
You could not hear a foot-fall
 Upon the yielding sod.
But she was filled with such delight —
 This foolish little Nell !
And with her fern-seed laden shoes,
 Danced back across the dell.
" I 'll find my mother now," she thought
 " What fun 't will be to call
' Mamma ! Mamma !' while she can see
 No little girl at all ! "
She peeped in through the window,
 Mamma sat in a dream :
About the quiet sun-steeped house
 All things asleep did seem.
She stept across the threshold ;
 So lightly had she crept,
The dog upon the mat lay still,
 And still the kitty slept.
Patient beside her mother's knee
 To try her wondrous spell
Waiting she stood, till all at once,
 Waking, mamma cried " Nell !
Where have you been ? why do you gaze

At me with such strange eyes?"
"But can you see me, mother dear?"
   Poor Nelly faltering cries.
"See you? why not, my little girl?
   Why should mamma be blind?"
And pretty Nell unties her shoes,
   With fairy fern-seed lined;
She tosses up into the air
   A little powdery cloud,
And frowns upon it as it falls,
   And murmurs half aloud,
"It was n't true, a word of it,
   About the magic spell!
I never will believe again
   What fairy stories tell!"

THE GREAT WHITE OWL.

He sat aloft on the rocky height,
  Snow-white above the snow,
In the winter morning calm and bright,
  And I gazed at him, below.

He faced the east, where the sunshine streamed
  On the singing, sparkling sea,
And he blinked with his yellow eyes, that seemed
  All sightless and blank to be.

The snow-birds swept in a whirling crowd
  About him gleefully,
And piped and whistled sweet and loud,
  But never a plume stirred he.

Singing they passed, and away they flew
  Through the brilliant atmosphere;
Cloud-like he sat, with the living blue
  Of the sky behind him, clear.

"Give you good-morrow, friend," I cried.
  He wheeled his large round head,
Solemn and stately, from side to side,
  But never a word he said.

"O lonely creature, weird and white,
  Why are you sitting there,
Like a glimmering ghost from the still midnight,
  In the beautiful morning air?"

He spurned the rock with his talons strong,
  No human speech brooked he;
Like a snow-flake huge he sped along
  Swiftly and noiselessly.

His wide, slow-waving wings so white,
  Heavy and soft did seem;
Yet rapid as a dream his flight,
  And silent as a dream.

And when a distant crag he gained,
  Bright-twinkling like a star,
He shook his shining plumes, and deigned
  To watch me from afar.

And once again, when the evening-red
  Burned dimly in the west,
I saw him motionless, his head
  Bent forward on his breast.

Dark and still, 'gainst the sunset sky
  Stood out his figure lone;
Crowning the bleak rock far and high,
  By sad winds overblown.

Did he dream of the ice-fields, stark and drear?
   Of his haunts on the Arctic shore?
Or the downy brood in his nest last year
   On the coast of Labrador?

Had he fluttered the Esquimaux huts among?
   How I wished he could speak to me!
Had he sailed on the icebergs, rainbow-hung,
   In the open Polar Sea?

Oh many a tale he might have told
   Of marvellous sounds and sights.
Where the world lies hopeless and dumb with
         cold,
   Through desolate days and nights.

But with folded wings, while the darkness fell,
   He sat, nor spake, nor stirred;
And charmed as if by a subtile spell,
   I mused on the wondrous Bird.

THE BLIND LAMB.

'T was summer, and softly the ocean
   Sang, sparkling in light and heat,
And over the water and over the land
   The warm south wind blew sweet.

And the children played in the sunshine,
   And shouted and scampered in glee
O'er the grassy slopes, or the weed-strewn beach,
   Or rocked on the dreaming sea.

They had roamed the whole bright morning,
   The troop of merry boys,
And in they flocked at noontide,
   With a clamor of joyful noise.

And they bore among them gently
   A wee lamb, white as snow ;
And, " O mamma, mamma, he 's blind !
   He can't tell where to go.

" And we found him lost and lonely,
   And we brought him home to you,
And we 're going to feed him and care for him ! "
   Cried the eager little crew.

"Look, how he falls over everything!"
 And they set him on his feet,
And aimlessly he wandered,
 With a low and mournful bleat.

Some sign of pity he seemed to ask,
 And he strove to draw more near,
When he felt the touch of a human hand,
 Or a kind voice reach his ear.

They tethered him in a grassy space
 Hard by the garden gate,
And with sweet fresh milk they fed him,
 And cared for him early and late.

But as the golden days went on,
 Forgetful the children grew,
They wearied of tending the poor blind lamb,
 No longer a plaything new.

And so each day I changed his place
 Within the garden fence,
And fed him morn and noon and eve,
 And was his Providence.

And he knew the rustle of my gown,
 And every lightest tone,
And when he heard me pass, straightway
 He followed o'er stock and stone.

One dark and balmy evening,
   When the south wind breathed of rain,
I went to lead my pet within,
   And found but a broken chain.

And a terror fell upon me,
   For round on every side
The circling sea was sending in
   The strength of the full flood-tide.

I called aloud and listened,
   I knew not where to seek;
Out of the dark the warm wet wind
   Blue soft against my cheek,

And naught was heard but the sound of waves
   Crowding against the shore.
Over the dewy grass I ran,
   And called aloud once more.

What reached me out of the distance?
   Surely, a piteous bleat!
I threw my long dress over my arm,
   And followed with flying feet.

Down to the edge of the water,
   Calling again and again,
Answered so clearly, near and more near,
   By that tremulous cry of pain!

4

I crept to the end of the rocky ledge,
  Black lay the water wide ;
Up from among the rippling waves
  Came the shivering voice that cried.

I could not see, but I answered him ;
  And, stretching a rescuing hand,
I felt in the darkness his sea-soaked wool,
  And drew him in to the land.

And the poor little creature pressed so close,
  Distracted with delight,
While I dried the brine from his dripping fleece
  With my apron soft and white.

Close in my arms I gathered him
  More glad than tongue can tell,
And he laid on my shoulder his pretty head,
  He knew that all was well.

And I thought as I bore him swiftly back,
  Content, close folded thus,
Of the Heavenly Father compassionate,
  Whose pity shall succor us.

I thought of the arms of mercy
  That clasp the world about,
And that not one of His children
  Shall perish in dread and doubt:

For He hears the voices that cry to Him,
  And near His love shall draw :
With help and comfort He waits for us,
  The Light, and the Life, and the Law!

DUST.

HERE is a problem, a wonder for all to see.
  Look at this marvellous thing I hold in my hand !
This is a magic surprising, a mystery
  Strange as a miracle, harder to understand.

What is it ? Only a handful of earth : to your touch
  A dry rough powder you trample beneath your feet,
Dark and lifeless ; but think for a moment, how much
  It hides and holds that is beautiful, bitter, or sweet.

Think of the glory of color ! The red of the rose,
  Green of the myriad leaves and the fields of grass,
Yellow as bright as the sun where the daffodil blows,
  Purple where violets nod as the breezes pass.

Think of the manifold form, of the oak and the vine,
  Nut, and fruit, and cluster, and ears of corn ;
Of the anchored water-lily, a thing divine,
  Unfolding its dazzling snow to the kiss of morn.

Think of the delicate perfumes borne on the gale,
  Of the golden willow catkin's odor of spring,
Of the breath of the rich narcissus waxen-pale,
  Of the sweet pea's flight of flowers, of the nettle's
    sting.

Strange that this lifeless thing gives vine, flower,
    tree
  Color and shape and character, fragrance too ;
That the timber that builds the house, the ship for
    the sea,
  Out of this powder its strength and its toughness
    drew !

That the cocoa among the palms should suck its milk
  From this dry dust, while dates from the self-same
    soil
Summon their sweet rich fruit : that our shining silk
  The mulberry leaves should yield to the worm's
    slow toil.

How should the poppy steal sleep from the very
    source
  That grants to the grape-vine juice that can mad-
    den or cheer ?
How does the weed find food for its fabric coarse
  Where the lilies proud their blossoms pure uprear ?

Who shall compass or fathom God's thought pro-
    found ?
  We can but praise, for we may not understand ;
But there 's no more beautiful riddle the whole world
    round
  Than is hid in this heap of dust I hold in my
    hand.

THE SCARECROW.

THE farmer looked at his cherry-tree,
  With thick buds clustered on every bough;
" I wish I could cheat the robins," said he;
  "If somebody only would show me how!

"I 'll make a terrible scarecrow grim,
  With threatening arms and with bristling head,
And up in the tree I 'll fasten him
  To frighten them half to death," he said.

He fashioned a scarecrow tattered and torn —
  Oh, 't was a horrible thing to see!
And very early, one summer morn,
  He set it up in his cherry-tree.

The blossoms were white as the light sea-foam,
  The beautiful tree was a lovely sight,
But the scarecrow stood there so much at home
  All the birds flew screaming away in fright.

The robins, who watched him every day,
  Heads held aslant, keen eyes so bright!
Surveying the monster, began to say,
  " Why should this monster our prospects blight ?

"He never moves round for the roughest weather,
   He 's a harmless, comical, tough old fellow ;
Let 's all go into the tree together,
   For he won't budge till the fruit is mellow!"

So up they flew ; and the sauciest pair
   Mid the shady branches peered and perked,
Selected a spot with the utmost care,
   And all day merrily sang and worked.

And where do you think they built their nest?
   In the scarecrow's pocket, if you please,
That, half-concealed on his ragged breast,
   Made a charming covert of safety and ease !

By the time the cherries were ruby-red,
   A thriving family, hungry and brisk,
The whole long day on the ripe fruit fed ;
   'T was so convenient! They ran no risk !

Until the children were ready to fly,
   All undisturbed they lived in the tree ;
For nobody thought to look at the Guy
   For a robin's flourishing family !

THE CRADLE.

THE barn was low and dim and old,
  Broad on the floor the sunshine slept,
And through the windows and the doors
  Swift in and out the swallows swept.

And breezes from the summer sea
  Drew through, and stirred the fragrant hay
Down-dropping from the loft, wherein
  A gray old idle fish-net lay

Heaped in a corner, and one loop
  Hung loose the dry, sweet grass among,
And hammock-wise to all the winds
  It floated to and fro, and swung.

And there one day the children brought
  The pet of all the house to play;
A baby boy of three years old,
  And sweeter than the dawn of day.

They laid him in the dropping loop,
  And softly swung him, till at last
Over his beauty balmy Sleep
  Its delicate enchantment cast.

And then they ran to call us all:
   "Come, see where little Rob is! Guess!"
And brought us where the darling lay,
   A heap of rosy loveliness

Curled in the net: the dim old place
   He brightened; like a star he shone
Cradled in air; we stood as once
   The shepherds of Judea had done.

And while adoring him we gazed,
  With eyes that gathered tender dew,
Wrathful upon the gentle scene
  His Celtic nurse indignant flew.

" Is this a fit place for the child ! "
  And out of his delicious sleep
She clutched him, muttering as she went,
  Her scorn and wonder, low and deep.

His father smiled, and drew aside ;
  A grave, sweet look was in his face,
" For One, who in a manger lay,
  It was not found too poor a place ! "

MARCH.

I WONDER what spendthrift chose to spill
Such bright gold under my window-sill ! \
Is it fairy gold ? Does it glitter still ?
Bless me ! it is but a daffodil !

And look at the crocuses, keeping tryst
With the daffodil by the sunshine kissed !
Like beautiful bubbles of amethyst
They seem, blown out of the earth's snow-mist.

And snow-drops, delicate, fairy bells,
With a pale green tint like the ocean swells;
And the hyacinths weaving their perfumed spells!
The ground is a rainbow of asphodels!

Who said that March was a scold and a shrew?
Who said she had nothing on earth to do
But tempests and furies and rages to brew?
Why, look at the wealth she has lavished on you!

O March that blusters and March that blows,
What color under your footsteps glows!
Beauty you summon from winter snows,
And you are the pathway that leads to the rose.

THE SHAG.

"WHAT is that great bird, sister, tell me,
   Perched high on the top of the crag?"
"'T is the cormorant, dear little brother:
   The fishermen call it the shag."

"But what does it there, sister, tell me,
   Sitting lonely against the black sky?"
"It has settled to rest, little brother;
   It hears the wild gale wailing high."

"But I am afraid of it, sister,
   For over the sea and the land
It gazes, so black and so silent!"
   "Little brother, hold fast to my hand."

"Oh what was that, sister? The thunder?
   Did the shag bring the storm and the cloud,
The wind and the rain and the lightning?"
   "Little brother, the thunder roars loud.

"Run fast, for the rain sweeps the ocean;
   Look! over the light-house it streams;
And the lightning leaps red, and above us
   The gulls fill the air with their screams."

THE SHAG

O'er the beach, o'er the rocks, running swiftly,
   The little white cottage they gain ;
And safely they watch from the window
   The dance and the rush of the rain.

But the shag kept his place on the headland,
   And when the brief storm had gone by,
He shook his loose plumes, and they saw him
   Rise splendid and strong in the sky.

Clinging fast to the gown of his sister,
   The little boy laughed as he flew :
" He is gone with the wind and the lightning !
   And — I am not frightened, — are you ? "

SIR WILLIAM NAPIER AND LITTLE JOAN.

SIR WILLIAM NAPIER, one bright day,
  Was walking down the glen,
A noble English soldier,
  And the handsomest of men.

Among the fragrant hedgerows
  He slowly wandered down,
Through blooming field and meadow,
  By pleasant Freshford town.

With look and mien magnificent
  And step so grand moved he!
And from his stately front outshone
  Beauty and majesty.

About his strong white forehead
  The rich locks thronged and curled
Above the splendor of his eyes
  That might command the world!

A sound of bitter weeping
  Came up to his quick ear,
He paused that instant, bending
  His kingly head to hear.

Among the grass and daisies
  Sat wretched little Joan,
And near her lay a bowl of delf
  Broken upon a stone.

Her cheeks were red with crying,
  And her blue eyes dull and dim,
And she turned her pretty woful face
  All tear stained up to him.

Scarce six years old and sobbing
  In misery so drear!
" Why, what's the matter, Posy ? "
  He said, " Come, tell me, dear."

" It 'sfather's bowl I 'se broken,
  'T was for his dinner kept :
I took it safe, but coming home
  It fell," — again she wept.

" But you can mend it, can't you ? "
  Cried the despairing child
With sudden hope, as down on her
  Like some kind god he smiled.

" Don't cry, poor little Posy !
  I cannot make it whole,
But I can give you sixpence
  To buy another bowl."

5

He sought in vain for silver
　　In purse and pockets too,
And found but golden guineas;
　　He pondered what to do.

"This time to-morrow, Posy,"
　　He said, "again come here,
And I will bring your sixpence.
　　I promise! Never fear!"

Away went Joan rejoicing.
　　A rescued child was she,
And home went good Sir William,
　　And to him presently

A footman brings a letter.
　　And low before him bends,
"Will not Sir William come and dine
　　To-morrow with his friends?"

The letter read, "And we've secured
　　The man among all men
You wish to meet! He will be here;
　　You will not fail us then?"

To-morrow! could he get to Bath
　　And dine with Dukes and Earls
And back in time? That hour was pledged —
　　It was the little girl's!

He could not disappoint her,
    He must his friend refuse,
So "a previous engagement"
    He pleaded as excuse.

Next day when she, all eager,
    Came o'er the fields so fair,
Not surer of the sunrise
    Than that she should find him there,

He met her, and the sixpence
    Laid in her little hand.
Her woe was ended, and her heart
    The lightest in the land.

How would the stately company
    Who had so much desired
His presence at their splendid feast,
    Have wondered and admired!

As soldier, scholar, gentleman,
    His praises oft are heard —
'T was not the least of his great deeds
    So to have kept his word.

BLUEBIRDS IN AUTUMN.

THE morning was gray and cloudy,
  And over the fading land
Autumn was casting the withered leaves
  Abroad with a lavish hand.

Sad lay the tawny pastures,
  Where the grass was brown and dry ;
And the far-off hills were blurred with mist,
  Under the sombre sky.

The frost already had fallen,
  No bird seemed left to sing ;
And I sighed to think of the tempests
  Between us and the spring.

But the woodbine yet was scarlet
  Where it found a place to cling ;
And the old dead weeping-willow
  Was draped like a splendid king.

Suddenly out of the heavens,
  Like sapphire sparks of light,
A flock of bluebirds swept and lit
  In the woodbine garlands bright.

The tree was alive in a moment
  With motion, color, and song ;
How gorgeous the flash of their azure wings
  The blood-red leaves among !

Beautiful, brilliant creatures !
  What sudden delight they brought
Into the pallid morning,
  Rebuking my dreary thought !

Only a few days longer,
  And they would have flown, to find
The wonderful, vanished summer,
  Leaving darkness and cold behind.

Oh, to flee from the bitter weather,
  The winter's buffets and shocks, —
To borrow their strong, light pinions,
  And follow their shining flocks !

While they sought for the purple berries,
  So eager and bright and glad,
I watched them, dreaming of April,
  Ashamed to have been so sad.

And I thought, "Though I cannot follow them,
  I can patiently endure,
And make the best of the snow-storms,
  And that is something more.

"And when I see them returning,
　　All heaven to earth they 'll bring;
And my joy will be the deeper,
　　For I shall have earned the spring."

TRAGEDY.

"You queer little wonderful owlet! you atom so
　　fluffy and small!
Half a handful of feathers and two great eyes — how
　　came you alive at all?
And why do you sit here blinking as blind as a bat
　　in the light,
With your pale eyes bigger than saucers? Now who
　　ever saw such a sight!

"And what ails chickadee, tell me! what makes him
　　flutter and scream
Round and over you where you sit like a tiny ghost
　　in a dream?
I thought him a sensible fellow, quite steady and
　　calm and wise,
But only see how he hops and flits, and hear how
　　wildly he cries!

"What is the matter, you owlet? You will not be
　　frightened away! —
Do you mean on that twig of a lilac-bush the whole
　　night long to stay?

Are you bewitching my chickadee-dee? I really be-
    lieve that you are!
I wish you 'd go off, you strange brown bird — oh,
    ever and ever so far!

"I fear you are weaving and winding some kind of
    a dreadful charm;
If I leave poor chickadee-dee with you, I 'm sure he
    will come to harm.
But what can I do? We can't stay here forever to-
    gether, we three —
One anxious child, and an owlet weird, and a fright-
    ened chickadee-dee!"

I could not frighten the owl away, and chickadee
    would not come,
So I just ran off with a heavy heart, and told my
    mother at home;
But when my brothers and sisters went the curious
    sight to see,
The owl was gone, and there lay on the ground *two
feathers* of chickadee-dee!

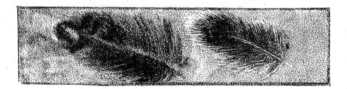

JACK FROST.

RUSTILY creak the crickets: Jack Frost came down
    last night,
He slid to the earth on a starbeam, keen and spark-
    ling and bright ;
He sought in the grass for the crickets with delicate
    icy spear,
So sharp and fine and fatal, and he stabbed them far
    and near.
Only a few stout fellows, thawed by the morning sun,
Chirrup a mournful echo of by-gone frolic and fun.
But yesterday such a rippling chorus ran all over the
    land,
Over the hills and the valleys, down to the gray sea-
    sand.
Millions of merry harlequins, skipping and dancing in
    glee,
Cricket and locust and grasshopper, happy as happy
    could be :
Scooping rich caves in ripe apples, and feeding on
    honey and spice,
Drunk with the mellow sunshine, nor dreaming of
    spears of ice !
Was it not enough that the crickets your weapon of
    power should pierce ?
Pray what have you done to the flowers ? Jack Frost,
    you are cruel and fierce.

With never a sign or a whisper, you kissed them,
    and lo, they exhale
Their beautiful lives ; they are drooping, their sweet
    color ebbs, they are pale,
They fade and they die !   See the pansies, yet striv-
    ing so hard to unfold
Their garments of velvety splendor, all Tyrian purple
    and gold.
But how weary they look, and   how withered, like
    handsome court dames, who all night
Have danced at the ball till the sunrise struck chill
    to their hearts with its light.
Where hides the wood-aster ?   She vanished as snow-
    wreaths dissolve in the sun
The moment you touched her.   Look yonder, where,
    sober and gray as a nun,
The maple-tree stands that at sunset was blushing as
    red as the sky ;
At its foot, glowing scarlet as fire, its robes of mag-
    nificence lie.
Despoiler ! stripping the world as you strip the shiv-
    ering tree
Of color and sound and perfume, scaring the bird
    and the bee,
Turning beauty to ashes — oh to join the swift swal-
    lows and fly
Far away out of sight of your mischief !   I give you
    no welcome, not I !

A LULLABY.

SLEEP, my darling, sleep!
    Thunders the pitiless storm;
    Fiercely at window and door
    Wrestle the winds and roar:
    Thy slumber is deep and warm.
Sleep, my darling, sleep!

Sleep, my baby, sleep!
    Over thy beautiful head,
    Lightly, softly, and close,
    Sweeter than lily or rose,
    Thy mother's kisses are shed.
Sleep, my baby, sleep!

Sleep, my darling, sleep!
    Safe in these arms, my own,
    Summer shall wrap thee round;
    Never harsh touch or sound
    Break through that charmèd zone.
Sleep, then, darling, sleep!

Sleep, my angel, sleep!
    Nestle against my heart,
    Sunk in a golden calm,—
    Delicate, breathing of balm,
    All my heaven thou art.
Sleep, my angel, sleep!

APRIL AND MAY.

I. APRIL.

BIRDS on the boughs before the buds
  Begin to burst in the Spring,
Bending their heads to the April floods,
  Too much out of breath to sing!

They chirp, " Hey-day ! How the rain comes down !
  Comrades, cuddle together !
Cling to the bark so rough and brown,
  For this is April weather.

"Oh, the warm, beautiful, drenching rain !
  I don't mind it, do you?
Soon will the sky be clear again,
  Smiling, and fresh, and blue.

" Sweet and sparkling is every drop
  That slides from the soft, gray clouds;
Blossoms will blush to the very top
  Of the bare old tree in crowds.

"Oh, the warm, delicious, hopeful rain !
  Let us be glad together.
Summer comes flying in beauty again,
  Through the fitful April weather."

II. MAY.

Skies are glowing in gold and blue ;
    What did the brave birds say ?
Plenty of sunshine to come, they knew,
    In the pleasant month of May !

She calls a breeze from the South to blow,
    And breathe on the boughs so bare,
And straight they are laden with rosy snow,
    And there's honey and spice in the air !

Oh, the glad, green leaves ! Oh, the happy wind !
    Oh, delicate fragrance and balm !
Storm and tumult are left behind
    In a rapture of golden calm.

From dewy morning to starry night
    The birds sing sweet and strong,
That the radiant sky is filled with light,
    That the days are fair and long.

That bees are drowsy about the hive —
    Earth is so warm and gay !
And 't is joy enough to be alive
    In the heavenly month of May !

APRIL AND MAY.

ROBIN'S RAIN-SONG.

O Robin, pipe no more of rain !
  'T is four days since we saw the sun,
And still the misty window pane
  Is loud with drops that leap and run.

Four days ago the sky was clear,
  But when my mother heard you call,
She said, "That 's Robin's rain-song, dear:
  Oh, well he knows when rain will fall !"

Fair was the morning, and I wept
  Because she would not let me stray
Into the woods for flowers, but kept
  My feet from wandering away.

And I was vexed to hear you cry
  So sweetly of the coming storm,
And watched with brimming eyes the sky
  Grow cold and dim from clear and warm.

It seemed to me you brought it all
  With that incessant, plaintive note ;
And still you call the drops to fall
  Upon your brown and scarlet coat.

How nice to be a bird like you,
  And let the rain come pattering down,
Nor mind a bit to be wet through,
  Nor fear to spoil one's only gown!

But since I cannot be a bird,
  Sweet Robin, pipe no more of rain!
Your merrier music is preferred;
  Forget at last that sad refrain!

And tell us of the sunshine, dear—
  I 'm wild to be abroad again,
Seeking for blossoms far and near:
  O Robin, pipe no more of rain!

A SONG OF EASTER.

    Sing, children, sing!
    And the lily censers swing;
Sing that life and joy are waking and that Death no
    more is king.
Sing the happy, happy tumult of the slowly brighten-
    ing Spring;
    Sing, little children, sing!

    Sing, children, sing!
    Winter wild has taken wing.

Fill the air with the sweet tidings till the frosty
    echoes ring!
Along the eaves the icicles no longer glittering cling,
And the crocus in the garden lifts its bright face to
    the sun,
And in the meadows softly the brooks begin to run.
      And the golden catkins swing
      In the warm airs of the Spring;
      Sing, little children, sing!

      Sing, children, sing!
      The lilies white you bring
In the joyous Easter morning for hope are blossom-
    ing;
And as the earth her shroud of snow from off her
    breast doth fling,
So may we cast our fetters off in God's eternal
    Spring.
So may we find release at last from sorrow and from
    pain,
So may we find our childhood's calm, delicious dawn
    again.
Sweet are your eyes, O little ones, that look with
    smiling grace,
Without a shade of doubt or fear into the future's face!

Sing, sing in happy chorus, with joyful voices tell
That death is life, and God is good, and all things
    shall be well;

6

That bitter days shall cease
In warmth and light and peace,
That Winter yields to Spring, —
Sing, little children, sing!

PERSEVERANCE.

Out I went in the morning, to look at my garden
    gay:
Everything shone with the dew-drops that sparkling
    and trembling lay
Scattered to left and to right, and the webs of the
    spiders were hung
Thickly with pearls and diamonds; light in the wind
    they swung.

Down in a corner, my sunflower, tall as a lilac-tree,
Shook out his tattered golden flags, and bowed and
    nodded to me.
Rather heavy-headed was he, for that I did not care,
For he blazed all over with flowers, though rather
    the worse for wear.

And under the sunflower, on the fence, a little brown
    bird sat,
Trying to sing; you never heard such a queer little
    song as that!

A soft brown baby sparrow, without any tail at all,
Trying his voice as he sat alone beneath the sunflower tall.

He could n't sing in the least, you know; he quavered and quavered again,
Seeking so hard to recollect his father's beautiful
strain!
But his young voice was hoarse and weak; he could
not find the tune
He used to hear above the nest in the happy days
of June.

But not at all was he daunted; he warbled it o'er
and o'er,
And every time I thought it grew more comical than
before.
The very sunflower seemed to laugh at the fluffy
little bird,
His broad, bright faces seemed to say, "Was ever
such music heard!"

I said, "Never mind, my darling; you'll conquer it
by and by,
For never baby or bird could fail, with so much
courage to try!"
So I left him there, still singing, and I heard him
every day
Doing bravely his little best, till winter drove him
away.

The dear bird and the golden flower! I mourned
　　when chilly snow
Sent south the small musician and laid the sunflower
　　low.
But I was sure, when in the spring the sparrows
　　should return,
His singing would be perfect, for he strove so hard
　　to learn.

RESCUED.

"Little lad, slow wandering across the sands so
　　yellow,
Leading safe a lassie small — Oh, tell me, little fel-
　　low,
Whither go you loitering in the summer weather,
Chattering like sweet-voiced birds on a bough to-
　　gether?"

"I am Robert, if you please, and this is Rose, my
　　sister,
Youngest of us all," — he bent his curly head and
　　kissed her;
"Every day we come and wait here till the sun is
　　setting,
Watching for our father's ship, for mother dear is
　　fretting.

" Long ago he sailed away out of sight and hearing,
Straight across the bay he went, into sunset steering.
Every day we look for him, and hope for his return-
    ing,
Every night my mother keeps the candle for him
    burning.

" Summer goes and Winter comes, and Spring re-
    turns, but never
Father's step comes to the gate. Oh! is he gone
    forever?
The great grand ship that bore him off, think you
    some tempest wrecked her?"
Tears shone in little Rose's eyes, upturned to her
    protector.

Eagerly the bonny boy went on: "Oh, sir, look
    yonder!
In the offing see the sails that east and westward
    wander;
Every hour they come and go, the misty distance
    thronging,
While we watch and see them fade, with sorrow and
    with longing."

" Little Robert! little Rose!" The stranger's eyes
    were glistening,
At his bronzed and bearded face upgazed the chil-
    dren, listening;

He knelt upon the yellow sand, and clasped them to
    his bosom,
Robert brave, and little Rose, as bright as any blos-
    som.

"Father! Father! Is it you?" The still air rings
    with rapture;
All the vanished joy of years the waiting ones re-
    capture!
Finds he welcome wild and sweet, the low-thatched
    cottage reaching,
But the ship that into sunset steered upon the rocks
    lies bleaching.

THE COCKATOOS.

EMPTY the throne-chair stood; mayhap
The king was taking his royal nap,
For early it was in the afternoon
Of a drowsy day in the month of June.

And the palace doors were open wide
To the soft and dreamful airs outside,
And the blue sky burned with the summer glow,
And the trees cool masses of shade did throw.

The throne-chair stood in a splendid room.
There were velvets in ruby and purple bloom,
Curtains magnificent to see,
And a table draped most sumptuously.

And on the table a cushion lay
Colored like clouds at the close of day,
And a crown, rich-sparkling with myriad rays,
Shone on the top in a living blaze.

And nobody spoke and nobody stirred
Except a bird that sat by a bird, —
Two cockatoos on a lofty perch,
Sober and grave as monks in a church.

Gay with the glory of painted plume
Their bright hues suited the brilliant room ;
Green and yellow, and rose and blue,
Scarlet and orange, and jet black, too.

Said one to the other, eyeing askance
The beautiful *fleur-de-lis* of France
On the cushion's lustrous edge, set round
In gleaming gold on a violet ground, —

Said one to the other, " Rocco, my dear,
If any thief were to enter here,
He might take crown and cushion away,
And who would be any the wiser, pray ? "

Said Rocco, " How stupid, my dear Coquette !
A guard is at every threshold set ;
No thief could enter, much less get out,
Without the sentinel's warning shout."

She tossed her head, did the bright Coquette.
" Rocco, my dear, now what will you bet
That the guards are not sleeping this moment as sound
As the king himself, all the palace round ?

" 'T is very strange, so it seems to me,
That they leave things open so carelessly ;
Really, I think it 's a little absurd
All this should be left to the care of a bird !

"And what is that creaking so light and queer?
Listen a moment. There! Don't you hear?
And what is that moving the curtain behind?
Rocco, my dear, are you deaf and blind?"

The heavy curtain was pushed away
And a shaggy head, unkempt and gray,
From the costly folds looked doubtful out,
And eagerly everywhere peered about.

And the dull eyes lighted upon the blaze
Of the gorgeous crown with a startled gaze,
And out of the shadow the figure stepped
And softly over the carpet crept.

And nobody spoke and nobody stirred,
And the one bird sat by the other bird,
Both overpowered by their surprise;
They really could n't believe their eyes!

Swiftly the madman, in fear's despite,
Darted straight to that hill of light;
The frightened birds saw the foolish wretch
His hand to the wondrous thing outstretch.

Then both at once such an uproar raised
That the king himself rushed in, amazed,
Half awake, in his dressing-gown,
And there on the floor lay the sacred crown!

And he caught a glimpse through the portal wide
Of a pair of flying heels outside,
And he shouted in royal wrath, "What ho!
Where are my people, I'd like to know!"

They ran to the rescue in terror great.
"Is this the way that you guard my state?
Had it not been for my cockatoos
My very crown I had chanced to lose!"

They sought in the shrubbery to and fro,
Wherever they thought the thief might go;
They looked through the garden, but all in vain,
They searched the forest, they scoured the plain.

They gave it up, for they could not choose.
But oh, the pride of those cockatoos!
If they were admired and petted before,
Now they were utterly spoiled, be sure!

They'd a special servant on them to wait,
To do their pleasure early and late:
They grew so haughty and proud and grand,
Their fame was spread over all the land.

And when they died it made such a stir!
And their skins were stuffed with spice and myrrh,
And from their perch they still look down,
As on the day when they saved the crown.

THE DOUBLE SUNFLOWER.

THE sunflowers hung their banners out in the sweet
    September weather ;
A stately company they stood by the garden fence
    together,
And looked out on the shining sea that bright and
    brighter grew,
And slowly bowed their golden heads to every wind
    that blew.

But the double sunflower bloomed apart, far prouder
    than the rest,
And by his crown's majestic weight he seemed almost
    oppressed.
He held himself aloof upon his tall and slender stem,
And gloried in the splendor of his double diadem.

All clothed in bells of lovely blue, a morning-glory
    vine
Could find no friendly stick or stalk about which she
    might twine ;
And prone upon the ground near by, with blossoms
    red as fire,
A scarlet runner lay for lack of means to clamber
    higher.

They both perceived the sunflower tall who proudly
    stood aside ;
Nothing to them was his grand air of majesty and
    pride ;
With one accord they charged at him, and up his
    stalk they ran,
And straight to hang their red and blue all over him
    began.

Oh, then he was magnificent, all azure, gold, and
    flame !
But, woe is me ! an autumn breeze from out the
    northwest came ;
With all their leaves and flowers the vines about him
    closely wound,
And with that keen wind's help at once they dragged
    him to the ground.

I found him there next morning, his pomp completely
    wrecked,
His prostrate form all gorgeously with tattered blooms
    bedecked.
"Alas !" I said, "no power on earth your glory can
    recall !
Did you not know, dear sunflower, that pride must
    have a fall ? "

I raised him up and bore him in, and, ere he faded
    quite,
In the corner he stood splendid awhile for our delight ;

But his humbler, single brethren, in the garden, every
      one,
With shining disks and golden rays stayed gazing at
      the sun.

IN THE BLACK FOREST.

Up through the great Black Forest,
  So wild and wonderful,
We climbed in the autumn afternoon
  'Mid the shadows deep and cool.

We climbed to the Grand Duke's castle
  That stood on the airy height;
Above the leagues of pine-trees dark
  It shone in the yellow light.

We saw how the peasant women
  Were toiling along the way,
In open spaces here and there,
  That steeped in the sunshine lay.

They gathered the autumn harvest —
  All toil-worn and weather-browned ;
They gathered the roots they had planted in spring,
  And piled them up on the ground.

We heard the laughter of children,
  And merrily down the road

Ran little Max with a rattling cart,
Heaped up with a heavy load.

———

Upon orange carrots, and beets so red,
 And turnips smooth and white,
With leaves of green all packed between,
 Sat the little Rosel bright.

Around the edge of her wee white cap
 The wind blew out her curls —
A sweeter face I have never seen
 Than this happy little girl's.

A spray of the carrot's foliage fine,
 Soft as a feather of green,
Drooped over her head from behind her ear
 As proud as the plume of a queen.

Light was his burden to merry Max,
 With Rosel perched above,
And he gazed at her on that humble throne
 With eyes of pride and love.

With joyful laughter they passed us by,
 As up through the forest of pine,
So solemn and still, we made our way
 To the castle of Eberstein.

Oh, vast and dim and beautiful
  Were the dark woods' shadowy aisles,
And all their silent depths seemed lit
  With the children's golden smiles.

Oh, lofty the Grand Duke's castle
  That looked o'er the forest gloom;
But better I love to remember
  The children's rosy bloom.

And sweet is the picture I brought away
  From the wild Black Forest shade,
Of proud and happy and merry Max,
  And Rosel, the little maid.

AN OLD SAW.

A DEAR little maid came skipping out
In the glad new day, with a merry shout;
With dancing feet and flying hair
She sang with joy in the morning air.

"Don't sing before breakfast, you'll cry before night!"
What a croak, to darken the child's delight!
And the stupid old nurse, again and again,
Repeated the ancient, dull refrain.

The child paused, trying to understand;
But her eyes saw the great world rainbow-spanned:
Her light little feet hardly touched the earth,
And her soul brimmed over with innocent mirth.

"Never mind, — don't listen, O sweet little maid!
Make sure of your morning song," I said;
"And if pain must meet you, why, all the more
Be glad of the rapture that came before."

AN OLD SAW.

CRADLE SONG.

In the wingèd cradle of sleep I lay
  My darling gently down ;
Kissed and closed are his eyes of gray,
  Under his curls' bright crown.

Where, oh where, will he fly and float,
  In the wingèd cradle of sleep?
Whom will he meet in the worlds remote,
  While he slumbers soft and deep ?

Warm and sweet as a white blush rose,
  His small hand lies in mine,
But I cannot follow him where he goes,
  And he gives no word nor sign.

Keep him safe ye heavenly powers,
  In dream-land vast and dim,
Let no ill, through the night's long hours,
  Come nigh to trouble him.

Give him back, when the dawn shall break,
  With his matchless baby charms,
With his love and his beauty all awake,
  Into my happy arms !

MARJORIE.

Marjorie hides in the deep, sweet grass;
  Purple its tops bend over;
Softly and warmly the breezes pass,
  And bring her the scent of the clover.

Butterflies flit, and the banded bee
  Booms in the air above her;
Green and golden lady-bugs three
  Marjorie's nest discover.

Up to the top of the grass so tall
  Creep they while Marjorie gazes;
Blows the wind suddenly — down they fall
  Into the disks of the daisies!

Brown-eyed Marjorie! Who, do you think,
  Sings in the sun so loudly?
Marjorie smiles. "'T is the bobolink,
  Carolling gayly and proudly."

Bright-locked Marjorie! What floats down
  Through the golden air, and lingers
Light on your head as a cloudy crown,
  Pink as your rosy fingers?

"Apple-blossoms!" she laughing cries,
  "Beautiful boats come sailing
Out of the branches held up to the skies,
  Over the orchard railing."

Happy, sweet Marjorie, hidden away,
  Birds, butterflies, bees above her;
With flowers and perfumes, and lady-bugs gay:
  Everything seems to love her!

KING MIDAS.

Heard you, O little children,
  This wonderful story told
Of the Phrygian king whose fatal touch
  Turned everything to gold?

In a great, dim, dreary chamber,
  Beneath the palace floor,
He counted his treasures of glittering coin,
  And he always longed for more.

When the clouds in the blaze of sunset
  Burned flaming fold on fold,
He thought how fine a thing 't would be
  Were they but real gold!

And when his dear little daughter,
  The child he loved so well,
Came bringing in from the pleasant fields
  The yellow asphodel,

Or buttercups from the meadow,
  Or dandelions gay,
King Midas would look at the blossoms sweet,
  And she would hear him say, —

" If only the flowers were really
　　Golden as they appear,
'T were worth your while to gather them,
　　My little daughter dear ! "

One day in the dim, drear chamber,
　　As he counted his treasure o'er,
A sunbeam slipped through a chink in the wall
　　And quivered down to the floor.

"Would it were gold," he muttered,
　　"That broad bright yellow bar ! "
Suddenly stood in its mellow light,
　　A figure bright as a star.

Young and ruddy and glorious,
　　With face as fresh as the day, .
With a wingèd cap and wingèd heels,
　　And eyes both wise and gay.

" Oh have your wish, King Midas,"
　　A heavenly voice begun,
Like all sweet notes of the morning
　　Braided and blended in one.

"And when to-morrow's sunrise
　　Wakes you with rosy fire,
All things you touch shall turn to gold,
　　Even as you desire."

King Midas slept. The morning
   At last stole up the sky,
And woke him, full of eagerness
   The wondrous spell to try.

And lo ! the bed's fine draperies
   Of linen fair and cool,
Of quilted satin and cobweb lace,
   And blankets of snowy wool,

All had been changed with the sun's first ray
   To marvellous cloth of gold,
That rippled and shimmered as soft as silk
   In many a gorgeous fold.

But all this splendor weighed so much
   'T was irksome to the king,
And up he sprang to try at once
   The touch on everything.

The heavy tassel that he grasped
   Magnificent became,
And hung by the purple curtain rich
   Like a glowing mass of flame.

At every step, on every side,
   Such splendor followed him,
The very sunbeams seemed to pale,
   And morn itself grow dim.

But when he came to the water
  For his delicious bath,
And dipped his hand in the surface smooth,
  He started in sudden wrath ;

For the liquid, light and leaping,
  So crystal-bright and clear,
Grew a solid lake of heavy gold,
  And the king began to fear !

But out he went to the garden,
  So fresh in the morning hour,
And a thousand buds in the balmy night
  Had burst into perfect flower.

'T was a world of perfume and color,
  Of tender and delicate bloom,
But only the hideous thirst for wealth
  In the king's heart found room.

He passed like a spirit of autumn
  Through that fair space of bloom,
And the leaves and the flowers grew yellow
  In a dull and senseless gloom.

Back to the lofty palace
  Went the glad monarch then,
And sat at his sumptuous breakfast,
  Most fortunate of men !

He broke the fine, white wheaten roll,
　The light and wholesome bread,
And it turned to a lump of metal rich —
　It had as well been lead!

Again did fear assail the king,
　When — what was this he heard?
The voice of his little daughter dear,
　As sweet as a grieving bird.

Sobbing she stood before him,
　And a golden rose held she,
And the tears that brimmed her blue, blue eyes
　Were pitiful to see.

"Father! O father dearest!
　This dreadful thing — oh, see!
Oh, what has happened to all the flowers?
　Tell me, what can it be?"

"Why should you cry, my daughter?
　Are not these' blossoms of gold
Beautiful, precious, and wonderful,
　With splendor not to be told?"

"I hate them, O my father!
　They 're stiff and hard and dead,
That were so sweet and soft and fair,
　And blushed so warm and red."

KING MIDAS.

"Come here," he cried, "my darling,"
 And bent, her cheek to kiss,
To comfort her — when — Heavenly Powers!
 What fearful thing was this?

He sank back, shuddering and aghast,
 But she stood still as death —
A statue of horrible gleaming gold,
 With neither motion nor breath.

The gold tears hardened on her cheek,
 The gold rose in her hand,
Even her little sandals changed
 To gold, where she did stand.

Then such a tumult of despair
 The wretched king possessed,
He wrung his hands, and tore his hair,
 And sobbed, and beat his breast.

Weighed with one look from her sweet eyes
 What was the whole world worth?
Against one touch of her loving lips,
 The treasure of all the earth?

Then came that voice, like music,
 As fresh as the morning air,
"How is it with you, King Midas,
 Rich in your answered prayer?"

And there, in the sunshine smiling,
    Majestic as before,
Ruddy and young and glorious,
    The Stranger stood once more.

"Take back your gift so terrible!"
    No blessing, but a curse!
One loving heart more precious is
    Than the gold of the universe."

The Stranger listened — a sweeter smile
    Kindled his grave, bright eyes.
"Glad am I, O King Midas,
    That you have grown so wise!

"Again your wish is granted;
    More swiftly than before,
All you have harmed with the fatal touch
    You shall again restore."

He clasped his little daughter —
    Oh, joy! — within his arms
She trembled back to her human self,
    With all her human charms.

Across her face he saw the life
    Beneath his kiss begin,
And steal to the charming dimple deep
    Upon her lovely chin.

Again her eyes grew blue and clear,
   Again her cheek flushed red,
She locked her arms about his neck,
   " My father dear!" she said.

Oh, happy was King Midas,
   Against his heart to hold
His treasure of love, more precious
   Than a thousand worlds of gold!

WILD GEESE.

THE wind blows, the sun shines, the birds sing loud,
The blue, blue sky is flecked with fleecy dappled
   cloud,
Over earth's rejoicing fields the children dance and
   sing,
And the frogs pipe in chorus, "It is spring! It is
   spring!"

The grass comes, the flower laughs where lately lay
   the snow,
O'er the breezy hill-top hoarsely calls the crow,
By the flowing river the alder catkins swing,
And the sweet song-sparrow cries, "Spring! It is
   spring!"

Hark, what a clamor goes winging through the sky!
Look, children! Listen to the sound so wild and
     high!
Like a peal of broken bells, — kling, klang, kling, —
Far and high the wild geese cry, "Spring! It is
     spring!"

Bear the winter off with you, O wild geese dear!
Carry all the cold away, far away from here;
Chase the snow into the north, O strong of heart and
     wing,
While we share the robin's rapture, crying, "Spring!
     It is spring!"

THE HYLAS.

In the crimson sunsets of the spring,
   Children, have you heard the hylas pipe,
Ere with robin's note the meadows ring,
   Ere the silver willow buds are ripe?

Long before the swallow dares appear,
   When the April weather frees the brooks,
Sweet and high a liquid note you hear,
   Sounding clear at eve from wooded nooks.

'T is the hylas. "What are hylas, pray?"
   Do you ask me, little children sweet?
They are tree-toads, brown and green and gray,
   Small and slender, dusky, light, and fleet.

All the winter long they hide and sleep
   In the dark earth's bosom, safe and fast;
When the sunshine finds them, up they leap,
   Glad to feel that spring is come at last.

Glad and grateful, up the trees they climb,
   Pour their cheerful music on the air,
Crying, "Here's an end of snow and rime!
   Beauty is beginning everywhere!"

8

Listen, children, for so sweet a cry!
  Listen till you hear the hylas sing,
Ere the first star glitters in the sky,
  In the crimson sunsets of the spring.

THE SPARROWS.

[DIE SPURVER.]

IN the far-off land of Norway,
  Where the winter lingers late,
And long for the singing-birds and flowers
  The little children wait;

When at last the summer ripens
  And the harvest is gathered in,
And food for the bleak, drear days to come
  The toiling people win;

Through all the land the children
  In the golden fields remain
Till their busy little hands have gleaned
  A generous sheaf of grain;

All the stalks by the reapers forgotten
  They glean to the very least,
To save till the cold December,
  For the sparrows' Christmas feast.

And then through the frost-locked country
  There happens a wonderful thing:
The sparrows flock north, south, east, west,
  For the children's offering.

Of a sudden, the day before Christmas,
  The twittering crowds arrive,
And the bitter, wintry air at once
  With their chirping is all alive.

They perch upon roof and gable,
  On porch and fence and tree,
They flutter about the windows
  And peer in curiously.

And meet the eyes of the children,
  Who eagerly look out
With cheeks that bloom like roses red,
  And greet them with welcoming shout.

On the joyous Christmas morning,
  In front of every door
A tall pole, crowned with clustering grain,
  Is set the birds before.

And which are the happiest, truly
  It would be hard to tell;
The sparrows who share in the Christmas cheer,
  Or the children who love them well!

How sweet that they should remember,
  With faith so full and sure,
That the children's bounty awaited them
  The whole wide country o'er!

When this pretty story was told me
  By one who had helped to rear
The rustling grain for the merry birds
  In Norway, many a year,

I thought that our little children
  Would like to know it too,
It seems to me so beautiful,
  So blessed a thing to do,

To make God's innocent creatures see
  In every child a friend,
And on our faithful kindness
  So fearlessly depend.

THE NIGHTINGALE.

THERE is a bird, a plain, brown bird,
    That dwells in lands afar,
Whose wild, delicious song is heard
    With evening's first white star.

When, dewy-fresh and still, the night
    Steals to the waiting world,
And the new moon glitters silver bright,
    And the fluttering winds are furled ;

When the balm of summer is in the air,
    And the deep rose breathes of musk,
And there comes a waft of blossoms fair
    Through the enchanted dusk ;

Then breaks the silence a heavenly strain,
    And thrills the quiet night
With a rich and wonderful refrain,
    A rapture of delight.

All listeners that rare music hail,
    All whisper softly: "Hark !
It is the matchless nightingale
    Sweet singing in the dark."

He has no pride of feathers fine;
  Unconscious, too, is he,
That welcomed as a thing divine
  Is his clear minstrelsy.

But from the fulness of his heart
  His happy carol pours;
Beyond all praise, above all art,
  His song to heaven soars.

And through the whole wide world his fame
  Is sounded far and near;
Men love to speak his very name;
  That brown bird is so dear.

GOLD LOCKS AND SILVER LOCKS.

Pupil and master together,
The wise man and the child
Merrily talking and laughing
Under the lamp-light mild.

Pupil and master together,
A fair sight to behold,
With his thronging locks of silver
And her tresses of ruddy gold.

"Well, little girl, did you practise
On the violin to-day?
What is the air I gave you?
Have you forgotten, pray?"

And he sings a few notes and pauses,
Half frowning to see her stand
Perplexed, with her white brows knitted,
And her chin upon her hand.

Far off in the street of a sudden
Comes the sound of a wandering band,
And the blare of brass rings faintly,
Too distant to understand.

"Hark!" says the master, smiling,
  Bending his head to hear,
"In what key are they playing?
  Can you tell me that, my dear?

"Is it D minor? Try it!
  To the piano and try!"
She strikes it, the sweet sound answers,
  Her touch so light and shy.

And swift as steel to magnet,
  The far tones and the near
Unite and are blended together
  Smoothly upon the ear.

I thought, if one had the power,
  What a beautiful thing 't would be,
Hearing Life's manifold music,
  To strike in one's self the key;

Whether joyful or sorry, to answer,
  As wind-harps answer the air,
And solve by simple submission
  Its riddles of trouble and care.

But the little maid knew nothing
  Of thoughts so grave and wise,
As she stole again to her teacher,
  And lifted her merry eyes.

GOLD LOCKS AND SILVER LOCKS.

And neither dreamed what a picture
They made, the young and the old, —
With his thronging locks of silver,
And her tresses of ruddy gold.

THE KITTIWAKES.

LIKE white feathers blown about the rocks,
   Like soft snow-flakes wavering in the air,
Wheel the Kittiwakes in scattered flocks,
   Crying, floating, fluttering everywhere.

Shapes of snow and cloud, they soar and whirl:
   Downy breasts that shine like lilies white;
Delicate vaporous tints of gray and pearl
   Laid upon their arching wings so light.

Eyes of jet, and beaks and feet of gold, —
   Lovelier creatures never sailed in air;
Innocent, inquisitive, and bold,
   Knowing not the dangers that they dare.

Stooping now above a beckoning hand,
   Following gleams of waving kerchiefs white,
What should they of evil understand,
   Though the gun awaits them full in sight?

Though their blood the quiet wave makes red,
    Though their broken plumes float far and wide,
Still they linger, hovering overhead,
    Still the gun deals death on every side.

Oh, begone, sweet birds, or higher soar!
    See you not your comrades low are laid?
But they only flit and call the more, —
    Ignorant, unconscious, undismayed.

Nay, then, boatman, spare them! Must they bear
    Pangs like these for human vanity?
That their lovely plumage we may wear
    Must these fair, pathetic creatures die?

Let the tawny squaws themselves admire,
    Decked with feathers — we can wiser be.
Ah, beseech you, boatman, do not fire!
    Stain no more with blood the tranquil sea.

LOST.

"*Lock the dairy door!*" Oh hark, the cock is crowing
    proudly!
"*Lock the dairy door!*" and all the hens are cack-
    ling loudly:
"*Chickle, chackle, chee,*" they cry ; "*we have n't got
    the key,*" they cry;
"*Chickle, chackle, chee! Oh dear, wherever can it be!*"
    they cry.

Up and down the garden walks where all the flow-
    ers are blowing,
Out about the golden fields where tall the wheat is
    growing,
Through the barn and up the road they cackle and
    they chatter:
Cry the children, "Hear the hens! Why, what can
    be the matter?"

What scraping and what scratching, what bristling
    and what hustling;
The cock stands on the fence, the wind his ruddy
    plumage rustling;
Like a soldier grand he stands, and like a trumpet
    glorious
Sounds his shout both far and near, imperious and
    victorious.

But to Partlets down below, who cannot find the key,
    they hear,
"*Lock the dairy door!*"   That 's all his challenge
    says to them, my dear.
Why they had it, how they lost it, must remain a
    mystery;
I that tell you, never heard the first part of the his-
    tory.

But if you will listen, dear, next time the cock crows
    proudly,
"*Lock the dairy door!*"   you 'll hear him tell the
    biddies loudly:
"*Chickle, chackle, chee,*" they cry; "*we have n't got
    the key!*" they cry;
"*Chickle, chackle, chee! Oh dear, wherever can it be!*"
    they cry.

THE KINGFISHER.

Could you have heard the kingfisher scream and scold
    at me
When I went this morning early down to the smiling
    sea!
He clamored so loud and harshly, I laughed at him
    for his pains,
And off he flew with a shattered note, like the sound
    of falling chains.

He perched on the rock above me, and kept up such
    a din,
He looked so fine with his collar snow-white beneath
    his chin,
And his cap of velvet, black and bright, and his jacket
    of lovely blue,
I looked, admired, and called to him, "Good morn-
    ing! How do you do?"

But his kingship was *so* offended! He had n't a
    pleasant word,
Only the crossest jargon ever screamed by a bird.
The gray sandpiper on one leg stood still in sheer
    surprise,
And gazed at me, and gazed at him, with shining
    bead-black eyes,

And pensively sent up so sweet and delicate a note,
Ringing so high and clear from out her dainty, mot-
    tled throat,
That echo round the silent shore caught up the clear
    refrain,
And sent the charming music back again, and yet
    again.

Then the brown song-sparrow on the wall made haste
    with such a song,
To try and drown that jarring din! but it was all
    too strong.

And the swallows, like a steel-blue flash, swept past
    and cried aloud,
"Be civil, my dear kingfisher, you 're far too grand
    and proud."

But it was n't of any use at all, he was too much
    displeased,
For only by my absence could his anger be appeased.
So I wandered off, and as I went I saw him flutter
    down,
And take his place once more upon the seaweed wet
    and brown.

And there he watched for his breakfast, all undis-
    turbed at last,
And many a little fish he caught as it was swimming
    past.
And I forgot his harsh abuse, for, up in the tall elm-
    tree,
A purple finch sat high and sang a heavenly song
    for me.

THE WOUNDED CURLEW.

By yonder sandy cove where, every day,
  The tide flows in and out,
A lonely bird in sober brown and gray
  Limps patiently about;

And round the basin's edge, o'er stones and sand,
  And many a fringing weed,
He steals, or on the rocky ledge doth stand,
  Crying, with none to heed.

But sometimes from the distance he can hear
  His comrades' swift reply;
Sometimes the air rings with their music clear,
  Sounding from sea and sky.

And then, oh then his tender voice, so sweet,
  Is shaken with his pain,
For broken are his pinions strong and fleet,
  Never to soar again.

Wounded and lame and languishing he lives,
  Once glad and blithe and free,
And in his prison limits frets and strives
  His ancient self to be.

9

The little sandpipers about him play,
  The shining waves they skim,
Or round his feet they seek their food, and stay
  As if to comfort him.

My pity cannot help him, though his plaint
  Brings tears of wistfulness ;
Still must he grieve and mourn, forlorn and faint,
  None may his wrong redress.

O bright-eyed boy! was there no better way
  A moment's joy to gain
Than to make sorrow that must mar the day
  With such despairing pain ?

O children, drop the gun, the cruel stone!
  Oh listen to my words,
And hear with me the wounded curlew moan —
  Have mercy on the birds!

LITTLE ASSUNTA.

CLIMBING the Pincian Hill's long slope,
    When the west was bright with a crimson flame,
Her small face glowing with life and hope,
    Little Assunta singing came.

From under ilex and olive-tree,
    I gazed afar to St. Peter's dome ;
Below, for a wondering world to see,
    Lay the ruined glories of ancient Rome.

Sunset was sorrowing over the land,
    O'er the splendid fountains that leaped in the air,
O'er crumbling tower and temple grand,
    Palace, and column, and statue fair.

Little Assunta climbed the steep ;
    She was a lovely sight to see !
A tint in her olive cheek as deep
    As the wild red Roman anemone.

Dark as midnight her braided hair
    Over her fathomless eyes of brown ;
And over her tresses the graceful square
    Of snow-white linen was folded down.

Her quaint black bodice was laced behind;
　Her apron was barred with dull rich hues;
Like the ripe pomegranate's tawny rind
　Her little gown; and she wore no shoes.

But round her dusk throat's slender grace,
　Large, smooth, coral beads were wound;
Like a flower herself in that solemn place
　She seemed, just blooming out of the ground.

Up she came, as she walked on air!
　I wandered downward with footsteps slow,
Till we met in the midst of the pathway fair,
　Bathed in the mournful sunset's glow.

"Buon giorno,[1] Signora!" she said;
　Like a wild-bird's note was her greeting clear.
"Salve!"[2] I answered, "my little maid;
　But 't is evening, and not good-morning, dear!"

She stretched her hands with a smile like light,
　As if she offered me, joyfully,
Some precious gift, with that aspect bright,
　And "Buon giorno!" again sang she.

---

[1] Good-morning, lady.

[2] A term of salutation pronounced "Salvé," and meaning "Hail," or "Welcome!"

LITTLE ASSUNTA.

And so she passed me and upward pressed
  Under ilex and olive-tree,
While the flush of sunset died in the west,
  And the shadows of twilight folded me.

She carried the morn in her shining eyes!
  Evening was mine, and the night to be;
But she stirred my heart with the dawn's surprise,
  And left me a beautiful memory!

INHOSPITALITY.

DOWN on the north wind sweeping
  Comes the storm with roaring din;
Sadly, with dreary tumult,
  The twilight gathers in.

The snow-covered little island
  Is white as a frosted cake;
And round and round it the billows
  Bellow, and thunder, and break.

Within doors the blazing drift-wood
  Is glowing, ruddy and warm,
And happiness sits at the fire-side,
  Watching the raging storm.

What fluttered past the window,
  All weary and wet and weak,

With the heavily drooping pinions,
　　And the wicked, crooked beak?

Cries the little sister, watching,
　　"Whither now can he flee?
Black through the whirling snow-flakes
　　Glooms the awful face of the sea,

"And tossed and torn by the tempest,
　　He must sink in the bitter brine!
Why could n't we pity and save him
　　Till the sun again should shine?"

They drew her back to the fireside,
　　And laughed at her cloudy eyes, —
"What, mourn for that robber-fellow,
　　The cruelest bird that flies!

"Your song-sparrow hardly would thank you,
　　And which is the dearest, pray?"
But she heard at the doors and windows
　　The lashing of the spray;

And as ever the shock of the breakers
　　The heart of their quiet stirred,
She thought, "Oh would we had sheltered him,
　　The poor, unhappy bird!"

Where the boats before the house-door
　　Are drawn up from the tide,

On the tallest prow he settles,
　And furls his wings so wide.

Uprises the elder brother,
　Uprises the sister too;
"Nay, brother, he comes for shelter!
　Spare him! What would you do?"

He laughs and is gone for his rifle.
　And steadily takes his aim;
But the wild wind seizes his yellow beard,
　And blows it about like flame.

Into his eyes the snow sifts,
　Till he cannot see aright:
Ah, the cruel gun is baffled!
　And the weary hawk takes flight;

And slowly up he circles,
　Higher and higher still;
The fierce wind catches and bears him away
　O'er the bleak crest of the hill.

UNDER THE LIGHT-HOUSE.

BENEATH the tall, white light-house strayed the children,
    In the May morning sweet ;
About the steep and rough gray rocks they wandered
    With hesitating feet ;
For scattered far and wide the birds were lying,
    Quiet, and cold, and dead,
That met, while they were swiftly winging northward,
    The fierce light overhead ;
And as the frail moths in the summer evenings
    Fly to the candle's blaze,
Rushed wildly at the splendor, finding only
    Death in those blinding rays.
And here were bobolink, and wren, and sparrow,
    Veery, and oriole,
And purple finch, and rosy grossbeak, swallows,
    And king-birds quaint and droll ;
Gay soldier blackbirds, wearing on their shoulders
    Red, gold-edged epaulets,
And many a homely, brown, red-breasted robin,
    Whose voice no child forgets.
And yellow-birds — what shapes of perfect beauty !
    What silence after song !
And mingled with them, unfamiliar warblers
    That to far woods belong.

Clothing the gray rocks with a mournful beauty
    By scores the dead forms lay,
That, dashed against the tall tower's cruel windows,
    Dropped like the spent sea spray.
How many an old and sun-steeped barn, far inland,
    Should miss about its eaves
The twitter and the gleam of these swift swallows!
    And, swinging 'mid the leaves,
The oriole's nest, all empty in the elm-tree,
    Would cold and silent be,
And never more these robins make the meadows
    Ring with their ecstasy.
Would not the gay swamp-border miss the blackbirds,
    Whistling so loud and clear?
Would not the bobolinks' delicious music
    Lose something of its cheer?
"Yet," thought the wistful children, gazing landward,
    "The birds will not be missed;
Others will take their place in field and forest,
    Others will keep their tryst:
And we, we only, know how death has met them;
    We wonder and we mourn
That from their innocent and bright existence
    Thus roughly they are torn."
And so they laid the sweet, dead shapes together,
    Smoothing each ruffled wing,
Perplexed and sorrowful, and pondering deeply
    The meaning of this thing.
(Too hard to fathom for the wisest nature
    Crowned with the snows of age!)

And all the beauty of the fair May morning
    Seemed like a blotted page.
They bore them down from the rough cliffs of granite
    To where the grass grew green,
And laid them 'neath the soft turf, all together,
    With many a flower between ;
And, looking up with wet eyes, saw how brightly
    Upon the summer sea
Lay the clear sunlight, how white sails were shining,
    And small waves laughed in glee :
And somehow, comfort grew to check their grieving,
    A sense of brooding care,
As if, in spite of death, a loving presence
    Filled all the viewless air.
"What should we fear ? " whispered the little children,
    "There is no thing so small
But God will care for it in earth or heaven :
    He sees the sparrows fall!"

PICCOLA.

Poor, sweet Piccola! Did you hear
What happened to Piccola, children dear?
'T is seldom Fortune such favor grants
As fell to this little maid of France.

'T was Christmas-time, and her parents poor
Could hardly drive the wolf from the door,
Striving with poverty's patient pain
Only to live till summer again.

No gifts for Piccola! Sad were they
When dawned the morning of Christmas-day;
Their little darling no joy might stir,
St. Nicholas nothing would bring to her!

But Piccola never doubted at all
That something beautiful must befall
Every child upon Christmas-day,
And so she slept till the dawn was gray.

And full of faith, when at last she woke,
She stole to her shoe as the morning broke;
Such sounds of gladness filled all the air,
'T was plain St. Nicholas had been there!

In rushed Piccola sweet, half wild:
Never was seen such a joyful child.
"See what the good saint brought!" she cried,
And mother and father must peep inside.

Now such a story who ever heard?
There was a little shivering bird!
A sparrow, that in at the window flew,
Had crept into Piccola's tiny shoe!

"How good poor Piccola must have been!"
She cried, as happy as any queen,
While the starving sparrow she fed and warmed,
And danced with rapture, she was so charmed.

Children this story I tell to you,
Of Piccola sweet and her bird, is true.
In the far-off land of France, they say,
Still do they live to this very day.

MOZART AT THE FIRESIDE.

Autumn nights grow chilly:
  See how faces bloom
By the cheerful fire-light,
  In the quiet room!

Mother's amber necklace,
  Father's beard of gold,
Rosy cheeks of little boys
  All glowing from the cold,

Basket heaped with barberries,
  Coral red and bright,
Little Silver's shaggy fur
  All shining in the light!

Barberries bright they 're picking,
  And smile and do not speak;
Happy little youngest boy
  Kisses mother's cheek, —

First mother's and then father's,
  And nestles his pretty head
In the shining fur of Silver,
  While they pick the barberries red.

10

At the piano sitting,
  One touches the beautiful keys ;
Silent they sit and listen
  To magical melodies.

Heavenly, tender, and hopeful,
  Balm for the saddest heart,
Rises the lovely music
  Of the divine Mozart !

The children hear the birds sing,
  And the voices of the May ;
They feel the freshness of morning,
  Before the toil of the day ;

But father and mother listen
  To a deeper undertone,
A strong arm, full of comfort, seems
  About life's trouble thrown.

O children, when your summer
  Passes, and winter is near,
When the sky is dim that was so bright,
  And the way seems long and drear,

Remember the mighty master
  Still touches the human heart,
Speaking afar from heaven,
  The wonderful Mozart !

He can bring back your childhood
  With his strains of airy grace,
Till life seems fresh and beautiful
  Again for a little space :

. With voices of lofty sweetness
  He shall encourage you,
Till all good things seem possible,
  And Heaven's best promise true ; .

Till health and strength and loveliness
  Blossom from stone and clod,
And the sad old world grows bright again
  With the cheerfulness of God.

THE FLOCK OF DOVES.

THE world was like a wilderness
  Of soft and downy snow;
The trees were plumed with feathery flakes,
  And the ground was white below.

Came the little mother out to the gate
  To watch for her children three ;
Her hood was red as a poppy-flower,
  And rosy and young was she.

She took the snow in her cunning hands,
  As waiting she stood alone,
And lo! in a moment, beneath her touch,
  A fair white dove had grown.

A flock she wrought, and on the fence
  Set them in bright array,
With folded wings, or pinions spread,
  Ready to fly away.

And then she hid by the pine-tree tall,
  For the children's tones rang sweet,
As home from school, through the drifts so light,
  They sped with merry feet.

"O Nannie, Nannie! See the fence
  Alive with doves so white!"
"Oh, hush! don't frighten them away!"
  They whisper with delight.

They crept so soft, they crept so still,
  The wondrous sight to see;
The little mother pushed the gate,
  And laughed out joyfully.

She clasped them close, she kissed their cheeks,
  And lips so sweet and red.
"The birds are only made of snow!
  You are my doves," she said.

THE FLOCK OF DOVES.

THE KAISERBLUMEN.

HAVE you heard of the Kaiserblume,
  O little children sweet,
That grows in the fields of Germany,
  Light waving among the wheat?

'T is only a simple flower,
  But were I to try all day,
Its grace and charm and beauty
  I could n't begin to say.

By field and wood and roadside,
  Delicate, hardy, and bold,
It scatters in wild profusion
  Its blossoms manifold.

The children love it dearly,
  And with dancing feet they go
To seek it with song and laughter ;
  And all the people know

Stern Kaiser Wilhelm loves it ;
  He said, "It shall honored be,
Henceforth 't is the Kaiserblume,
  The flower of Germany."

Then he bade his soldiers wear it,
  Tied in a gay cockade,
And the quaint and humble blossom
  His royal token made.

Said little Hans to Gretchen,
  One summer morning fair,
As they played in the fields together,
  And sang in the fragrant air :

" Oh look at the Kaiserblumen
  That grow in the grass so thick !
Let's gather our arms full, Gretchen,
  And take to the Emperor, quick !

"For never were any so beautiful,
  Waving so blue and bright."
So all they could carry they gathered,
  Dancing with their delight.

Then under the blazing sunshine
  They trudged o'er the long, white road
That led to the Kaiser's palace,
  With their gayly nodding load.

But long ere the streets of the city
  They trod with their little feet,
As hot they grew and as tired
  As their corn flowers bright and sweet.

And Gretchen's cheeks were rosy
  With a weary travel stain,
And her tangled hair o'er her blue, blue eyes
  Fell down in a golden rain.

And at last all the nodding blossoms
  Their shining heads hung down;
But, "Cheer up, Gretchen!" cried little Hans,
  We 've almost reached the town.

"We 'll knock at the door of the palace,
  And won't he be glad to see
The flowers we 've brought so far for him?
  Think, Gretchen, how pleased he 'll be!"

So they plodded patiently onward,
  And with hands so soft and small
They knocked at the palace portal,
  And sweetly did cry and call:

"Please open the door, O Kaiser!
  We 've brought some flowers for you,
Our arms full of Kaiserblumen,
  All gay and bright and blue!"

But nobody heeded or answered,
  Till at last a soldier grand
Bade the weary wanderers leave the gate,
  With a gruff and stern command.

But, "No!" cried the children, weeping;
  Though trembling and sore afraid,
And clasping their faded flowers,
  "We *must* come in!" they said.

A lofty and splendid presence
  The echoing stair came down;
To know the king there was no need
  That he should wear a crown.

And the children cried: "O Kaiser,
  We have brought your flowers so far!
And we are so tired and hungry!
  See, Emperor, here they are!"

They held up their withered posies,
  While into the Emperor's face
A beautiful light came stealing,
  And he stooped with a stately grace;

Taking the ruined blossoms,
  With gentle words and mild
He comforted with kindness
  The heart of each trembling child.

And that was a wonderful glory
  That the little ones befell!
And when their heads are hoary,
  They still will the story tell,

How they sat at the Kaiser's table,
  And dined with princes and kings,
In that far off day of splendor,
  Filled full of marvellous things!

And home, when the sun was setting,
  The happy twain were sent,
In a gleaming golden carriage,
  With horses magnificent.

And like the wildest vision
  Of fairy-land it seemed;
Hardly could Hans and Gretchen
  Believe they had not dreamed.

And even their children's children
  Eager to hear will be,
How they carried to Kaiser Wilhelm
  The flowers of Germany.

Printed in Great Britain
by Amazon

38277980R00096